# LATIN
## FOR BEGINNERS

Angela Wilkes

Illustrated by John Shackell

Designed by Roger Priddy

Language consultants: Graham Tingay and Rubricastellanus
(Karl-Heinz Graf von Rothenburg)

Edited by Jane Chisholm

## CONTENTS

Latin was the language of the Ancient Romans. Although Romans nowadays speak Italian instead, Latin is still spoken in schools and universities all over the world. It is the official language of the Catholic Church. Scientists use Latin for classifying and naming new species, and scholars even get together to agree on "new" Latin words for ordinary things, like *television* and *pizza*, that didn't exist in Roman times.

## You can find out how to ...

talk about yourself,

and your home and family,

count and tell the time,

ask for the food you like,

find your way around,

and go shopping.

## How you learn

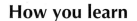

salve!

salve!

hic Petrus est.

The pictures show you what to say in each situation. Read the speech bubbles, and see how much you can understand by yourself. Then look up any words you do not know. Words and phrases are repeated again and again, to help you remember them. The book starts with things that are easy to say and gets harder as you go on.

2

## New words

New words are listed on each double page, so you can find them as you go along. If you forget a word, you can look it up on pages 46-48. An asterisk* by a word means there is a note about it at the bottom of the page. The Romans did not use capital letters at the beginning of a sentence, except for names.

## Grammar

Latin is easier if you know some of its grammar, or rules, but it doesn't matter if you don't understand it all straightaway. Boxes like this around words show where new grammar is explained. You can look up any of the grammar, including the rules about how Latin word endings change, on pages 41-43.

## Internet links*

At the top of each double page you will find descriptions of useful websites for learning Irish. For links to these sites, go to **www.usborne-quicklinks.com** and enter the keywords **Irish for beginners**.

## Puzzles

Throughout this book there are puzzles and quizzes to solve (see answers on pages 44-45). You can also find picture puzzles to print out on the Usborne Quicklinks Website at **www.usborne-quicklinks.com**

## Practising your Latin

Write all the new words in a notebook, and try to learn a few every day. Keep going over them and you will soon remember them.

Ask a friend or someone in your family to test you. Better still, find someone to learn Latin with you, so you can test each other.

requiro . . .

Try speaking in Latin whenever you can. Don't be afraid of making mistakes. Look out for Latin written in old buildings or churches.

* For more information on using the Internet, see inside the front cover.

# Saying "Hello" and "Goodbye"

The first thing you should know how to say in Latin is "Hello". Here you can find out how to greet people at different times of day.

**salve/salvete**\*\*    hello
**bonum diem**    good day
**bonam vésperum**    good evening
**bonam noctem**    goodnight
**vale/valete**\*\*    goodbye

It is polite to add **domine** (Sir) for a man, **domina** (Madam) for a woman, and **dominula** (Miss) for a girl.

## Saying "Hello"

This is how you say "Hello" to a friend.

**bonum diem** means "Good day!".

This is how you say "Good evening".

## Saying "Goodbye"

**salve** can mean "Goodbye" as well as "Hello".

**vale** means "Goodbye" and "Farewell".

## Saying "Goodnight"

You only use **bonam noctem** last thing at night.

## How are you?

This means "How are you?".

This woman is saying that she is fine, thank you....

...but this man is saying that he isn't very well.

### ut vales?

What do you think these people would say if you asked them how they were? Choose from the list below.

| | |
|---|---|
| **ut vales?** | how are you? |
| **bene váleo** | I'm fine, well |
| **grátias ago** | thank you |
| **óptime** | very well |
| **bene** | well |
| **satis bene** | quite well |
| **non ita bene** | not very well |
| **péssime** | terrible |

5

# What is your name ?

Here you can find out how to ask someone their name and tell them yours, and how to introduce your friends. Read the picture strip and see how much you can understand. Then try doing the puzzles on the page opposite.

## New words

| | |
|---|---|
| **quod nomen tibi est ?** | what's your name? |
| **mihi nomen est** | my name is |
| **quod est nomen amícae meae?** | what is my friend's name? |
| **nomen meum** | my name |
| **nomen tuum** | your name |
| **nomen eius** | his/her name |
| **nómina eorum** | their names |
| **amícus meus est** | he is my friend |
| **amíca mea** | my (girl) friend |
| **quis?** | who? |
| **hic puer** | this boy |
| **haec puélla** | this girl |
| **et tibi?** | and you? |
| **quis est hic /haec\*?** | who is this (boy/girl)? |
| **quod ... est?** | what is...? |
| **quae ... sunt?** | what are...? |
| **ita est!** | so it is / yes |
| **non** | not |
| **sed** | but |
| **sunt** | (they) are |

## Questions

Questions in Latin sometimes have a questioning word at the beginning, such as **quis** (who?), **cur** (why?), **quando** (when?), or **ut** (how?). If there is no questioning word, **-ne** is added to the end of the first word. This shows that the sentence is a question. For example, **"estne nomen eius Petrus?"** means "Is his name Peter?".

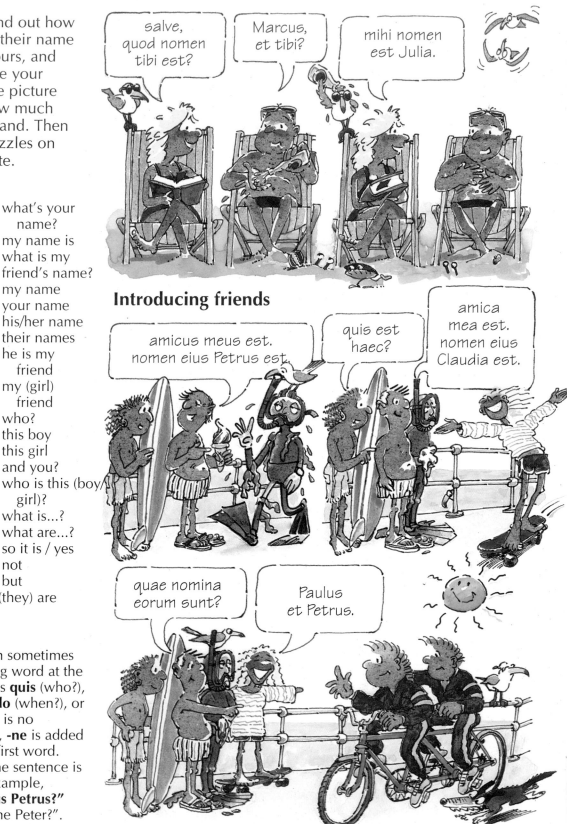

**Introducing friends**

* To find out more about **hic** and **haec**, see page 8.

## What are they called?

Can you answer these questions in Latin?

quod est nomen amicae meae?

quod nomen tibi est?

quod nomen eius est?

quae nomina eorum sunt?

## Who is who?

Can you answer the questions below the picture?

salve, ut vales?

bene valeo, gratias ago.

vale, Carole.

estne haec puella Cornelia?

ita est! nomen eius Cornelia est.

valo.

nomen eius Quintus est.

quis est hic puer?

mihi nomen Marcus non est, sed Lucius.

estne tibi nomen Marcus?

quod nomen tibi est?

Beata, et tibi?

Who is talking to Quintus?
Who is talking to Beata?

Which person is Lucius?
Who is speaking to him?

Who is reading the paper?
Who is going home?

## Can you remember?

How would you ask someone's name?
How would you tell them your name?

You have a friend called Beata.
How would you introduce her?
How would you tell someone that your friend's name is Gaius?

# Finding out what things are called

Everything on this picture has its name on it. See if you can learn the names for everything, then try the quiz in the box at the bottom of the opposite page.

caminus(m)

tectum(n)

sol(m)

avis(f)

salvete!

nidus(m)

arbor(f)

fenestra(f)

flos(m)

domus(f)

haec domus mea est.

porta(f)

stabulum autocineticum(n)

saeptum(n)

canis(m)

feles(f)

autocineticum(n)

## Nouns

All Latin nouns are either masculine, feminine or neuter (neither). This is called their gender. The gender is shown in the word lists by the letters m, f and n. Many masculine nouns end in **-us**, feminine nouns in **-a** and neuter nouns in **-um**. But there are many exceptions and many other endings too. There is no way of guessing the gender of most things. You just have to learn them. The endings of words also change according to how they are used. The different endings, called cases, will be explained later.

There is no word in Latin for "the" or "a", but you can often use the word "this" instead: **hic** (m), **haec** (f), **hoc** (n). **hic** and **haec** can sometimes be used to mean "he" and "she".

**quid hoc est?**      what is this?
**hic/haec/hoc est...**   this is...

# New words

| | |
|---|---|
| **étiam** | also |
| **arbor (f)** | tree |
| **domus (f)** | house |
| **cáminus (m)** | chimney |
| **avis (f)** | bird |
| **tectum (n)** | roof |
| **Latíne/Anglice** | in Latin/English |
| **fenéstra (f)** | window |
| **flos (m)** | flower |
| **porta (f)** | door |
| **canis (m)** | dog |
| **feles (f)** | cat |
| **nidus (m)** | nest |
| **sol (m)** | sun |
| **autocinéticum (n)** | car |
| **stábulum autocinéticum (n)** | |
| | garage |
| **saeptum (n)** | fence |

quid hoc est?

hic flos est.

etiamne flos est?

non flos sed arbor est.

quid est hoc Latine?

haec est porta.

et quid hoc est?

hic canis est.

quid est hoc Anglice?

A dog.

## Can you remember?

Cover up the word lists, and see if you can name these things in Latin. Begin your answers with **hic est**, **haec est** or **hoc est**.

9

# Where do you come from?

Here you can find out how to ask people where they come from. You can also find out if they can speak Latin.

## New Words

| | |
|---|---|
| **unde venis?** | where do you come from? |
| **vénio e/ex** | I come from... |
| **ubi hábitas?** | where do you live? |
| **hábito (in)** | I live in... |
| **loquor** | I speak |
| **scio** | I know (how to) |
| **scisne loqui...?** | can you speak...? |
| **paulum** | a little |
| **Latíne** | (in) Latin |
| **Gállice** | (in) French |
| **Germánice** | (in) German |
| **Ánglice** | (in) English |
| **ecce** | here is... |
| **et** | and |
| **-que** (on the end of a word) | and |
| **Lóndinii** | in London |
| **Lutétiae** | in Paris |
| **Gállia** | France |
| **Caledónia** | Scotland |
| **Hispánia** | Spain |
| **Germánia** | Germany |
| **Itália** | Italy |
| **Hungária** | Hungary |

## Where do you come from?

unde venis?

e Britannia venio.

ubi habitas?

Londinii habito.

unde venis?

e Germania venio.

amica mea e Gallia venit, et Lutetiae habitat.

## Can you speak Latin?

scisne loqui Latine?

Latine paulum loqui scio.

scisne loqui Latine, Octavia?

loquor Latine et paulum Anglice.

Henricus scit loqui Latine et Anglice et Germanice.

# Who comes from where?

These are the contestants for an international dancing competition. They have come from all over the world. The organizer cannot speak any Latin and does not understand where anyone comes from. Read about the contestants, then see if you can tell him what he wants to know. His questions are beneath the picture.

Angus
e Caledonia
venit.

ecce Maria
et Petrus!
e Gallia
veniunt.

Arius et Indira
ex India veniunt.

Ianus ex
Hungaria venit.
habitat
Aquinci.

Franciscus ex
Austria venit.

ecce Lolita!
ex Hispania
venit.

Where do they all come from?

Where does Franz (Franciscus) come from?
What are the names of the Indians?
Is Lolita Italian or Spanish?
Who lives in Budapest (Aquincum)?

Is there a Scottish contestant?
Where do Marie and Pierre (Maria and Petrus) come from?
Where is Budapest?

## Verbs (action words)

Latin verbs change their endings according to who is doing the action. Verbs ending in **-are** follow the same pattern as **habitare**. Verbs ending in **-ire** (such as **scire**) are like **venire**.

| habitare | to live in | venire | to come |
|---|---|---|---|
| **habit-o*** | I live in | **veni-o** | I come |
| **habit-as** | you live in | **veni-s** | you come |
| **habit-at** | he/she lives in | **veni-t** | he/she comes |
| **habit-amu**s | we live in | **veni-mus** | we come |
| **habit-atis** | you live in | **veni-tis** | you come |
| **habit-ant** | they live in | **veni-unt** | they come |

## Can you remember?

How would you ask someone where they come from?
How do you say that you can speak Latin?

Can you say where you come from?
How do you ask someone else if they can speak Latin?

---

*In Latin you do not need a separate word for "I", "you", "we" etc. There is more about verbs on pages 41 and 42.  11

# More about you

Here you can find out how to say how old you are, how many brothers and sisters you have, and how to count up to 20.

In Latin, a boy says **decem annos natus sum** for "I am ten years old", and a girl says **decem annos nata sum**.

## New words

| | |
|---|---|
| **quot?** | how many? |
| **quot annos?** | how many years? |
| **natus, -a, -um** | born |
| **tu** | you (singular) |
| **mihi est/sunt...** | I have... |
| **tibi est/sunt...** | you have... |
| **frater meus** | my brother |
| **fratres** | brothers |
| **soror mea** | my sister |
| **soróres** | sisters |
| **paene** | almost, nearly |
| **neque...neque** | neither...nor |

## Describing words

The endings of Latin adjectives change according to the word they describe. For example, in the singular you use **natus** for masculine words, **nata** for feminine words and **natum** for neuter words. In the plural, the masculine is **nati**, the feminine is **natae** and the neuter is **nata**.

## Numbers*

1 **unus, una, unum**
2 **duo, duae, duo**
3 **tres, tres, tria**
4 **quáttuor**
5 **quinque**
6 **sex**
7 **septem**
8 **octo**
9 **novem**
10 **decem**

## How old are you?

## Have you any brothers or sisters?

*There is a longer list of numbers on page 40.

## How old are they ?

Read what these children are saying, then see if you can say how old they are.

> Titus duodecim annos natus est.

> quindecim annos natae sumus.

> Livia undecim annos nata est.

> Afer paene quattuordecim annos natus est.

> quinque annos nata sum, hic novem annos natus est.

Afer     Diana et Sylvia     Titus     Livia     Lucius   Aemilia

## Brothers and sisters

Below you can read how many brothers and sisters the children have. Can you work out who has which brothers and sisters?

**Dianae et Sylviae unus frater et duo sorores sunt.**

**Liviae tres sorores et duo fratres sunt.**

**Afro quinque sorores, sed fratres non sunt.**

**Lucio unus frater est, sed sorores non sunt.**

**Tito neque fratres neque sorores sunt, sed canis ei est.**

## The verb "to be"

| | |
|---|---|
| **esse** | to be |
| **sum** | I am |
| **es** | you are |
| **est** | he/she/it is |
| **sumus** | we are |
| **estis** | you are (plural) |
| **sunt** | they are |

## The dative

| | |
|---|---|
| **mihi** | to me |
| **tibi** | to you |
| **ei** | to him |
| **Lucio** | to Lucius |

The Latin for "Titus has one brother" is **est Tito unus frater**, which literally means "To Titus is one brother". This uses the dative case, shown here.

# Talking about your family

You will find lots of words on these two pages to help you talk about your family.

Many of the phrases include the words "my" and "your", which you first learned on page 12.

ecce familia mea.

canis meus

meus avus

meus pater

soror mea

patruus meus

feles mea

avia mea

mater mea

frater meus

amita mea

## Who's who?

estne hic frater tuus?

ita est. frater meus est.

estne haec soror tua?

ita est. nomen eius Licinia est.

suntne hi parentes tui?

minime! avus et avia sunt.

## New words

| | | | | | |
|---|---|---|---|---|---|
| família (f) | family | ego | I | parvus, -a, -um | little |
| paréntes (m) | parents | nos | we | crassus, -a, -um | fat |
| pater (m) | father | avúnculus (m) | uncle | grácilis, -is, -e | thin |
| mater (f) | mother | pátruus (m) | uncle | flavus, -a, -um | blonde, yellow |
| avus (m) | grandfather | ámita (f) | aunt | fuscus, -a, -um | dark |
| ávia (f) | grandmother | matértera (f) | aunt | tener, -era, -erum | gentle |
| | | magnus, -a, -um | large | vetérrimus, -a, -um | very old |

## "My" and "your"

The words for "my" and "your" vary, just like other adjectives. They have to agree with the gender and number of the noun (whether it is singular or plural).

| | masculine | feminine | neuter |
|---|---|---|---|
| my (singular) | meus | mea | meum |
| your (singular) | tuus | tua | tuum |
| my (plural) | mei | meae | mea |
| your (plural) | tui | tuae | tua |

## Describing your family

pater meus magnus,
sed mater mea
parva est.

mater mea magna,
sed pater
meus parvus est.

patruus meus crassus,
sed amita mea
gracilis est.

avus meus
veterrimus est.
ego parvus sum.

soror mea
flava est.
frater meus
fuscus est.

canis meus
tener est.

## Describing words

As you learned on page 12, Latin adjectives* change their endings according to the gender of the word they are describing. Many end in **-us**, **-a**, **-um**. Some others end in **-is**, **-is**, **-e** in the singular, and **-es**, **-es**, **-ia** in the plural.

Can you describe each of these people in Latin, using the new words you have learned. Start with **hic** or **haec est**...?

* You can find out more about adjectives on page 43.

# Your home

Here you can find out how to say what sort of home you live in, and where it is. You can also learn what all the rooms are called.

## New words

| | |
|---|---|
| **aut** | or |
| **domus (f)** | house |
| **ínsula (f)** | block of flats |
| **palátium (n)** | palace |
| **in urbe** | in the city |
| **ruri** | in the country |
| **ad mare** | at, by the sea |
| **papa (m)** | Dad |
| **mamma (f)** | Mum/Mom |
| **larva (f)** | ghost |
| **ubi es/estis?** | where are you? |
| **bálneum (n)** | bath |
| **cenáculum (n)** | dining-room |
| **cubículum (n)** | bedroom |
| **mediánum (n)** | living room |
| **coquína (f)** | kitchen |
| **vestíbulum (n)** | hall |
| **tabulátum (n)** | storey |
| **in summo tabuláto** | on the top storey |
| **hábito** | I live in |

## Where do you live?

> habitasne in domo aut insula?

> in domo habito.

> in insula habito.

> in palatio habito.

## Town or country?

> in urbe habito.

> ruri habito.

> ad mare habito.

## Where is everyone?

Dad comes home and wants to find out where everyone is. Look at the pictures and see if you can tell him. (For example, **avia in mediano est.**)

Then see if you can answer the questions below the little pictures.

mater     pater     avus

avia     Petrus     Isabella

Quintus     larva

**quis in cenaculo est?**
**quis in coquina est?**
**quis in balneo est?**
**quis in cubiculo est?**

**ubi avia est?**
**ubi larva est?**
**ubi Isabella est?**
**ubi Petrus est?**

## Can you remember?

Cover up the pictures and see if you can remember how to say these things. The answers are on page 44.

I live in a town. You live in the country.
The bedroom is on the top storey.

Grandma lives in a block of flats.
Quintus is in the bath.
We live in a house.

# Looking for things

Here you can find out how to ask someone what they are looking for and tell them where things are. You can also learn lots of words for things around the house.

## New words

| | |
|---|---|
| quaero | I look for |
| quaeris | you look for |
| áliquid | something |
| cricétus (m) | a hamster |
| repério | I find |
| eum/eam/id | him/her/it |
| in armário | in/on the cupboard |
| sub sponda | under the sofa |
| post velum | behind the curtain |
| inter plantas | among the plants |
| sponda (f) | sofa |
| sella (f) | chair |
| velum (n) | curtain |
| planta (f) | plant |
| mensa (f) | table |
| librárium (n) | bookcase |
| tapéte (n) | carpet |
| televisórium (n) | television |
| telephónum (n) | telephone |
| vásculum (n) | vase |

## Prepositions

| | |
|---|---|
| ad | at, to, by the side of (+ acc.) |
| ab | by, from (+ abl.) |
| ante | in front of (+ acc.) |
| e, ex | out of (+ abl.) |
| in | in (+ abl.), into (+ acc.) |
| post | behind, after (+ acc.) |
| prope | near (+ acc.) |
| sub | under (+ acc. & abl.) |

The accusative case* for nouns ending in **-us** or **-um** is **-um**, and the ablative case is **-o**. For nouns ending in **-a**, the accusative is **-am** and the ablative is **-a**.

## The missing hamster

quaerisne aliquid?

cricetum meum quaero. eum reperire non possum!

in armario non est.

etiam sub sponda non est.

estne post velum?

minime!

ecce! inter plantas est!

*You can find out more about cases on page 42.

## In, on or under?

**in cista** means "in the box". What do the other phrases mean? See how the ending of **cista** changes with the different prepositions.

in cista   post cistam   ante cistam   ad cistam   sub cista   in cista

## Where are the animals hiding?

Grandfather's six pets are hiding somewhere in the room. Can you tell him where they are, using the prepositions above and giving each noun the right ending?

cricetus

feles parva

canicula

psittacus

serpens

testudo

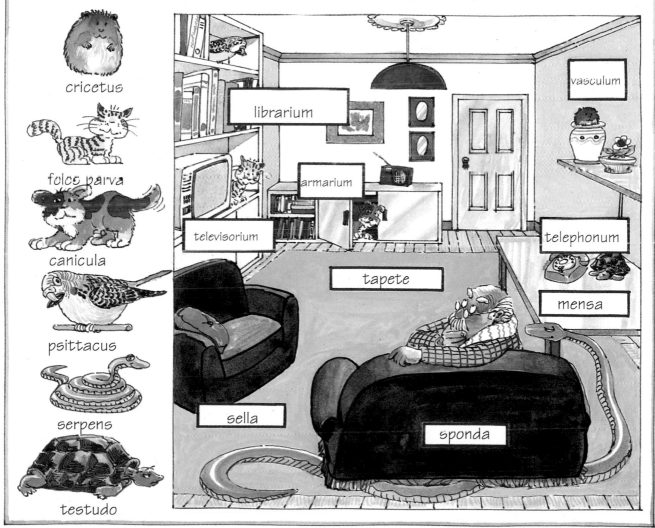

librarium

vasculum

armarium

televisorium

telephonum

tapete

mensa

sella

sponda

19

# What do you like eating?

Here you can learn lots of food words and find out how to say what you like and don't like.

## New words

| | |
|---|---|
| amare | to like, love |
| amo | I like |
| amas | you like |
| amat | he/she likes |
| quid? | what? |
| quid ergo? | what then? |
| valde | very much |
| mínime | not at all |
| tum | then |
| máxime | most, best |
| praéfero | I prefer |
| edo | I eat |
| ego quoque | I also |
| láctuca (f) | lettuce |
| piscis (m) | fish |
| poma terréstria assa (n.pl) | chips |
| placénta (f) | cake |
| bótulus (m) | sausage |
| búbula assa (f) | steak |
| pasta vermiculáta (f) | spaghetti |
| pitta (f) | pizza |
| Hammaburgénsis (m) | hamburger |
| óryza (f) | rice |
| panis (m) | bread |
| cáseus (m) | cheese |
| scriblíta (f) | a tart |

## What would you like?

amasne lactucam?

lactucam non amo.

amasne piscem?

minime!

quid ergo amas?

amo poma terrestria assa.

valde placentam amo.

## What do you like most ?

quid maxime amas?

valde botulum amo.

sed bubulam assam praefero...

pastam vermiculatam amo.

20

*Internet link:* For links to websites where you can find ancient Roman recipes and more Latin food words, go to **www.usborne-quicklinks.com**

# What are they eating?

quid edis?

pittam edo.

poma terrestria assa edit.

panem et caseum edit.

Hammabergenses edimus.

oryzam editis.

bananas edunt.

## Who likes what ?

Who likes cheese ? Who likes ham? Who prefers grapes to bananas?

Can you say in Latin which things you like and which you don't like?

ego quoque, sed pernam non amo.

bananas amo.

sed ego uvas praefero.

Marcus

caseum amo.

Julius

avus

maxime amo scriblitam pomorum.

Henricus

perna      butyrum

scriblita casei

Julia

panis      lactuca      tomatae      caseus

bananae      uvae      scriblita pomorum      aranciata

## Subject and object

In the sentence **avus pernam amat** ("Grandfather likes ham."), **avus** is the subject and **pernam** is the object. In Latin, the subject uses the nominative case*, which

is the one we use when talking about a noun. The object uses the accusative case. This is why when Henricus says **caseum amo** ("I love cheese"), **caseum** is in the accusative.

*You can find more about different cases on pages 42-43.

21

# Table talk

Here you can learn about things to say during a meal.

## New words

| | |
|---|---|
| **veníte ad mensam!** | come to the table! |
| **quaeso** | I beg/please |
| **esúrio** | I am hungry |
| **sume áliquid!** | Take something! |
| **bene tibi sápiat!** | Bon appetit! |
| **sapítne bene?** | Does it taste good? |
| **óptime** | excellent |
| **potésne mihi dare...** | Can you give me... |
| **aqua/aquam (acc.) (f)** | water |
| **panis/panem (acc.) (m)** | bread |
| **hýalus/hýalum (acc.) (m)** | a glass |
| **caro/carnem (acc.) (f)** | meat |
| **visne áliquid?** | Would you like anything? |
| **volo** | I wish, want |
| **vis** | you wish, want |
| **etiam** | also |
| **nolo** | I don't want |
| **satis** | enough |
| **estne bonum?** | Is it good? |
| **óptimum est!** | It's very good! |

## Dinner is ready

venite ad mensam!

esurio.

ego quoque.

sume aliquid, quaeso!

gratias ago.

bene tibi sapiat!

bene tibi sapiat!

## Please will you pass me...

da mihi aquam, quaeso.

da mihi panem, quaeso.

da mihi hyalum, quaeso.

# Would you like some more?

## Who is saying what ?

These little pictures show different mealtime situations. Cover up the rest of the page and see if you know what each of them would say in Latin.

Julius is crying that he is hungry.

The chef wants you to enjoy your meal.

Julia is saying "Help yourself".

Peter wants someone to give him a glass.

Julius's mother asks him if he wants more chips.

He says "Yes, please", and that he likes chips.

Then he says "No thanks", he's had enough.

Mark is saying the food tastes delicious.

## Nouns and cases

Here are the endings of most of the nouns and cases you have met so far. Another group of nouns ends in **-em** in the accusative singular, and **-es** in the accusative plural.

| Singular | | | | Plural | | | |
|------|------|------|------|------|------|------|------|
| Nom. | **-us** | **-a** | **-um** | Nom. | **-i** | **-ae** | **-a** |
| Acc. | **-um** | **-am** | **-um** | Acc. | **-os** | **-as** | **-a** |
| Dat. | **-o** | **-ae** | **-o** | Dat. | **-is** | **-is** | **-is** |

23

# Your hobbies

These people are talking about their hobbies.

## New words

| | |
|---|---|
| **píngere** | to paint |
| **cóquere** | to cook |
| **mihi placet...** | I like to... |
| **plassáre** | to make models |
| **saltáre** | to dance |
| **légere** | to read |
| **spectáre** | to watch/look at |
| **téxere** | to weave/knit |
| **natáre** | to swim |
| **audíre** | to listen to |
| **athlética (f)** | sport |
| **cánere** | to play (an instrument) |
| **lúdere** | to play (a game) |
| **pedifóllis (m)** | football |
| **tenilúdium (n)** | tennis |
| **música (n.pl)** | music |
| **instruméntum músicum (n)** | musical instrument |
| **violína (f)** | violin |
| **clavárium (n)** | piano |
| **vésperi** | in the evening |
| **sóleo...** | I usually |
| **libri (m.pl)** | books |

## More verbs

Two different types of verb endings were shown on page 11. Here are two more.

| | |
|---|---|
| **placere*** | to please |
| | |
| **plac-eo** | I please |
| **plac-es** | you please |
| **plac-et** | he/she/it pleases |
| **plac-emus** | we please |
| **plac-etis** | you please |
| **plac-ent** | they please |
| | |
| **ludere*** | to play |
| | |
| **lud-o** | I play |
| **lud-is** | you play |
| **lud-it** | he/she/it plays |
| **lud-imus** | we play |
| **lud-itis** | you play |
| **lud-unt** | they play |

quid tibi facere placet?

pingere mihi placet.

sed coquere mihi non placet.

quid ergo tibi placet?

mihi placet plassare.

mihi placet saltare.

## What do you do in the evenings?

quid vesperi facis?

aut libros legere...

...aut televisorium spectare et texere soleo.

*placere rhymes with "airy". **ludere** rhymes with "prudery".

## The sporty type

quid tibi placet?

athletica mihi placet.

mihi natare placet.

ego pedifolle ludo.

et ego teniludio ludo.

## Music lovers

quid vobis placet?

nobis musica audire placet.

canitisne instrumentis musicis?

clavario cano.

ita est. violina cano.

## What are they doing?

A

B

C

D

E

Can you say in Latin what these people are doing? (E.g. A: **hic coquit**.) How would you ask the cook what he is doing? What would he answer? And the others?

25

# Telling the time

Here you can find out how to tell and ask the time in Latin. For "one o'clock" in Latin, you would say **prima hora** (first hour).

The Ancient Romans divided the day in a different way from us. You can find out how they told the time on page 48.

## New words

| | |
|---|---|
| **dic mihi** | tell me |
| **quota hora est?** | What is the time? |
| **prima hora est.** | It's one o'clock. |
| **secúnda hora est.** | It's two o'clock. |
| **quinque minútae ante/post +acc.** | five minutes to/past... |
| **quadrans ante/ post + acc.** | a quarter to../ past... |
| **quadránte...** | at a quarter... |
| **tértia hora et dimídia** | half past three |
| **merídies (m)** | midday, noon |
| **média nox (f)** | midnight |
| **mane (n)** | (in the) morning |
| **súrgere** | to rise, get up |
| **ientáculum (n)** | breakfast |
| **prándium (n)** | lunch |
| **cena (f)** | dinner, supper |
| **in scholam ire** | to go to school |
| **dórmitum ire** | to go to bed |

## First, second, third...

| | | | |
|---|---|---|---|
| 1st | **primus,** | **-a,** | **-um** |
| 2nd | **secúndus,** | **-a,** | **-um** |
| 3rd | **tértius,** | **-a,** | **-um** |
| 4th | **quartus,** | **-a,** | **-um** |
| 5th | **quintus,** | **-a,** | **-um** |
| 6th | **sextus,** | **-a,** | **-um** |
| 7th | **séptimus,** | **-a,** | **-um** |
| 8th | **octávus,** | **-a,** | **-um** |
| 9th | **nonus,** | **-a,** | **-um** |
| 10th | **décimus,** | **-a,** | **-um** |
| 11th | **úndecimus,** | **-a,** | **-um** |
| 12th | **dúodecimus,** | **-a,** | **-um** |

26

## What is the time?

This is how you ask the time.

## The time is...

quinque minutae sunt post nonam horam.

quadrans post nonam horam est.

nona hora est et dimidia.

quadrans ante decimam (horam)

quinque minutae ante decimam

meredies/media nox

## What time of day?

sexta hora ante meridiem est.

sexta hora post meridiem est.

## Marcus's day

Read what Marcus does during the day, then see if you can match each clock with the right picture. You can check your answers on page 45.

**1** Marcus surgit septima hora et dimidia.

**2** hora octava ientaculum sumit.

**3** quadrante ante novam in scholam it.

**4** duodecima et dimidia prandium sumit.

**5** decem minutis post secundam pedifolle ludit.

**6** quadrante post quintam televisorium spectat.

**7** sexta hora cenam sumit.

**8** octava hora et dimidia dormitum it.

## What is the time?

Can you say in Latin what times these clocks show?

# Arranging things

Here is how to arrange to do things with your friends.

## New words

| | |
|---|---|
| quando | when |
| usque ad + acc. | until... |
| post merídiem | in the afternoon |
| bene | good |
| hódie | today |
| vésperi | in the evening |
| cras (adverb) | tomorrow |
| dies crastínus (m) | tomorrow |
| possum | I can |
| potes | you can |
| adíre cínema | to go to the cinema |
| ádibis | you will go to |
| ludémus | we will play |
| natábimus | we will swim |
| convívium (n) | party |
| discothéca (f) | disco |
| saltáre | to dance |
| dóleo quod | I am sorry that |

## Days of the week

| | |
|---|---|
| dies Lunae | Monday |
| dies Martis | Tuesday |
| dies Mercúrii | Wednesday |
| dies Iovis | Thursday |
| dies Véneris | Friday |
| dies Satúrni | Saturday |
| dies Solis | Sunday |

## Tennis

## Swimming

## Going to the cinema

# Going to a party

> potesne adire convivium meum?

> quando?

> die Saturni vesperi.

> doleo, quod non possum.

> die Saturni discothecam adibo.

---

## Your diary for the week

This is your diary for the week. Read it and see if you can answer the questions.

What are you doing on Friday evening ?
When are you playing tennis ?
What are you doing on Tuesday afternoon?

**dies Lunae**
4.hora   teniludium

**dies Martis**
2.hora   clavarium
5.30     natare

**dies Mercurii**
3.hora   teniludium
7.45     cinema

**dies Iovis**

**dies Veneris**
8.hora   saltare cum Tito

**dies Saturni**
2.hora   pediludium
7.hora   convivium

**dies Solis**
post meridiem:
teniludium

## The ablative

The ablative is one of the six cases used with Latin nouns. It is used for time. For example **die** (abl.) **Lunae** means "on Monday". It is also used with prepositions. **in urbe** (abl.) means "in the city".

## The future

| | I shall... | you | he/she/it |
|---|---|---|---|
| **habitare** (to live): | **habitabo,** | -abis, | -abit* |
| **placere** (to please): | **placebo,** | -ebis, | -ebit |
| **ludere** (to play): | **ludam,** | -es, | -et |
| **venire** (to come): | **veniam,** | -ies, | -iet |

*You can find the future tense conjugated in full on page 42.

# Asking the way

The next three pages show you how to find your way around.

## New Words

| | |
|---|---|
| **da mihi véniam** | excuse me |
| **illic, ibi** | there |
| **nihil labóris est** | it's no trouble |
| **in diréctum** | straight ahead |
| **flecte te sinistrórsum** | turn (to the) left |
| **dextrórsum** | (to the) right |
| **deinde** | then |
| **a laeva parte** | on the left |
| **a dextra parte** | on the right |
| **officium postále (n)** | post office |
| **deversórium statiónis ferriviáriae (n)** | station hotel |
| **ubi est?** | where is? |
| **forum (n)** | market-place |
| **in propínquo** | nearby |
| **i, ibis** | go!, you will go |
| **estne longínquum?** | is it far? |
| **fere** | almost |
| **minúta (f)** | a minute |
| **pédibus** | on foot, walking |
| **cafea (f)** | café, coffee |
| **pharmacopóla (f)** | chemist, pharmacy |
| **argentária (f)** | bank |
| **contra** | against, opposite |
| **supermercátus (m)** | supermarket |

## Being polite

> da mihi veniam, domine...

> gratias ago.

> nihil laboris est.

To ask something politely, remember to add **domine**, **domina** or **dominula**.

If someone thanks you for something, it is polite to answer **nihil laboris est**.

## Where is...?

> da mihi veniam domina, ubi est officium postale?

> illic, in foro.

> ubi est, quaeso, deversorium stationis ferriviariae?

> flecte te sinistrorsum, deinde i in directum.

### Direction signs

**in directum**

**sinistrorsum**     **dextrorsum**

## Is there a . . . nearby?

## Is it far?

> da mihi veniam domine, estne cafea in propinquo?

> ita est. i sinistrorsum in viam poetae Ovidii.

> estne longinquum?

> mInIme, pedibis quinque minutas ibis.

> da mihi veniam dominula, estne supermercatus in propinquo?

> Ita est. illic contra argentariam.

> estne etlam pharmacopola in propinquo?

> ibi prope supermercatum.

## Other useful places to ask for

| statio ferriviaria | statio benzinaria | latrina | receptaculum epistularum |
|---|---|---|---|
| railway station | garage | toilet | postbox |
| cella telephonica | campus tentorius | valetudinarium | aeriportus |
| telephone box | camp site | hospital | airport |

31

# Finding your way around

Here you can find out how to ask your way around and follow directions. When you have read everything else, try the map puzzle on the opposite page.

## New words

| | | | |
|---|---|---|---|
| **qua via vénio ad..?** | how do I get to..? | **praefectúra commeátus (f)** | tourist office |
| **cape** | take | **cúria (f)** | town hall |
| **véhere** | drive! | **tabérna (f)** | shop |
| **autoraedáne?** | by car? | **piscína (f)** | swimming baths |
| **via prima** | first road | **deversórium (n)** | hotel |
| **via próxima** | next road | **ecclésia (f)** | church |
| **devertículum júvenum (n)** | youth hostel | **sita est** | is situated |

## The imperative form

The imperative is the part of the verb you use for giving orders. Here are some examples in the singular: **i** (go!), **veni** (come!), **flecte** (turn!), **cape** (take!), **vehere** (drive!) and **da** (give!). There is more about the imperative on page 41.

## Finding your way around Messina

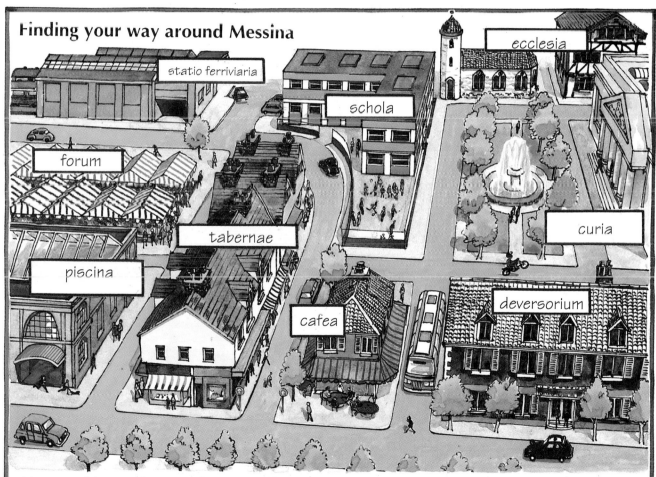

How would you ask someone the way to the market place? How would you ask if there is a café nearby?

Can you tell the driver of the red car how to get to the station? Then tell the driver of the yellow car how to get to the church.

Where would these directions take the yellow car?
**i secunda via sinistrorsum, deinde vehere semper in directum.**

# Going shopping

Here you can find out what to say in Latin when you go shopping.

## New words

| | |
|---|---|
| **émere** | to buy |
| **cibária (n.pl)** | food, provisions |
| **pistrína (f)** | bakery |
| **tabérna alimentária (f)** | grocer's |
| **laniéna (f)** | butcher's |
| **lac (n)** | milk |
| **ovum (n)** | egg |
| **pomum (n)** | fruit |
| **hólera (n.pl)** | vegetables |
| **caro (f)** | meat |
| **panicéllus (m)** | roll, bun |
| **malum (m)** | apple |
| **tomáta (f)** | tomato |
| **quid requíris?** | what do you want? |
| **pecúnia (f)** | money |
| **quid áliud?** | what else? |
| **quanti constant?** | how much do they cost? |
| **ómnia** | everything |
| **nihil iam** | nothing now |
| **libra (f)** | pound (weight) |

## Roman money

Throughout the long history of the Roman empire, the look and value of coins was always changing, just as they do today. The coins in use were:

**quadrans** (copper)
**semis** (copper) = **2 quadrántes**
**as** (copper) = **2 semísses**
**dupóndius** (copper) = **2 asses**
**sestértius** (copper) = **2 dupóndii**
**denárius** (silver) = **4 sestértii**
**aúreus** (gold) = **25 denárii**

Although it was not worth very much, the **sestertius** was the coin the Romans used most often when describing the value of something. It was rather like a British penny or US cent.

## Cornelia goes shopping

Cornelia cibaria emit.

in pistrina panem emit.

## In the baker's

salve, domina!

salve, domina!

ecce quattor panicelli. quid aliud?

nihil iam. quanti constant?

requiro quattor panicellos.

hi constant quinquaginta sestertiis*.

ecce pecunia! gratias!

*Internet link:* For a link to a website where you can learn new Latin words every week, go to **www.usborne-quicklinks.com**

**lac et ova in taberna alimentaria emit.**

**poma et holera in foro emit.**

**carnem in laniena emit.**

## At the grocer's

*At the grocer's speech bubbles:*

quid requiris?

requiro sex ova, quaeso.

quid aliud?

unam litram lactis, quaeso.

quanti constant haec omnia?

omnia constant centum viginti sestertiis.

## At the market

*At the market speech bubbles:*

salve, domina! quid requiris?

requiro duas libras malorum.

quid aliud?

unam libram tomatarum.

haec omnia octoginta* sestertiis.

*You will find a list of Latin numbers on page 40.

35

# Shopping and going to a café

Here you can find out how to ask how much things cost and how to order in a café.

## New words

| | |
|---|---|
| **chártula (f)** | postcard |
| **rosa (f)** | rose |
| **rátio/ratiónem (acc.f)** | bill |
| **aráncium (n)** | orange |
| **aranciáta (f)** | orange juice |
| **ananása (f)** | pineapple |
| **cítreum (n)** | lemon |
| **limonáta (f)** | lemonade |
| **pérsicum (n)** | peach |
| **cola (f)** | cola |
| **thea (f)** | tea |
| **cum lacte** | with milk |
| **cum citreo** | with lemon |
| **potus socolatae (m)** | drinking chocolate |
| **glácies (f)** | ice-cream |
| **velim** | I would like |
| **hyalus (m)** | a glass |
| **cafea (f)** | a café, coffee |
| **quanti constat...?** | how much does...cost? |
| **quanti constant..?** | how much do...cost? |

## Asking how much things cost

## Going to a café

## Buying fruit

Everything on the fruit stall is marked with its name and price. Look at the picture, then see if you can answer the questions below it.

MALA
libra
HS LV

quid
requiris?

BANANAE
libra
HS LVIII

UVAE
libra
HS CXX

ARANCIA
unum
HS XXII

ANANASAE
una
HS CX

PERSICA
libra
HS CCLX

CITREA
unum
HS XV

How do you tell the stallholder you would like four lemons, a pound of bananas and a pineapple? How much do each of these things cost? How much is the total?

**quid constat HS CX?**
**quid constat HS CCLX?**
**quanti constant tres aranciae?**
**quanti constat una libra malorum?**

## In the café

Here are some things you might order in a café.

velim...

| | | | |
|---|---|---|---|
| unam limonatam | unam colam | unam theam cum lacte | unam theam cum citreo |
| unam aranciatam | unum potum socolatae | unum hyalum lactis | unam glaciem |

# Months, seasons and dates

Here you can learn what the seasons and months are called and find out how to say what the date is.

## New Words

| | |
|---|---|
| **annus, anni (gen.m)** | year |
| **mensis, -sis (gen.m)** | month |
| **natális (m)** | birthday |
| **hódie** | today |
| **qui dies?** | what day? |
| **quando?** | when? |

## The seasons

| | |
|---|---|
| **ver (n)** | spring |
| **aestas (f)** | summer |
| **autúmnus (m)** | autumn |
| **hiems (f)** | winter |

## The months

| | |
|---|---|
| **Ianuárius, -arii** | January |
| **Februárius, -arii** | February |
| **Mártius, -tii** | March |
| **Aprílis, -is** | April |
| **Maius, -ii** | May |
| **Iúnius, -ii** | June |
| **Iúlius, -ii** | July |
| **Augústus, -i** | August |
| **Septémber, -bris** | September |
| **Octóber, -bris** | October |
| **Novémber, -bris** | November |
| **Decémber, -bris** | December |

## The seasons

ver

Martius, Aprilis, Maius

aestas

Iunius, Iulius, Augustus

autumnus

September, October, November

hiems

December, Ianuarius, Februarius...

## The genitive and ablative

The genitive case is used for "of..": e.g. **anni** (of the year). The ablative case is used for time and often means "on" or "at": e.g. **secundo die Maii** (on the second day of May). It is also used (often with prepositions) to mean "by", "with" or "from": e.g. **cum meo patre** (with my father) and **ex urbe** (from the city). Another use is for describing a position: e.g. **a sinistra parte** (on the left) and **in urbe** (in the city).

Ianuarius primus mensis anni est.

Februarius secundus mensis anni est.

December duodecimus mensis anni est.

Can you decribe the other months of the year in the same way?

# What is the date*?

> hodie tertius dies Maii est.

> qui dies hodie est?

> hodie primus dies Ianuarii est.

## Writing the date

Romae, die 3.° mensis Maii.

The little sign ° is the abbreviation of the ordinal number (first, second, third..). For example, 2.° is **secundo** (second).

# When is your birthday?

> quando tuus natalis est?

> die 10.° mensis Novembris.

> natalis meus est die 12.° mensis Februarii.

> natalis Iulii est die 8.° mensis Iunii.

# When are their birthdays?

The dates of the children's birthdays are written below their pictures. Can you say in Latin when they are (e.g. **natalis Carinae est die 2.° mensis Aprilis.**)?

| Carina | Robertus | Helena | Clara | Claudius | Leo |
|---|---|---|---|---|---|
| die 2.° m. Aprilis | die 21.° m. Iunii | die 18.° m. Octobris | die 31.° m. Augusti | die 3.° m. Martii | die 7.° m. Septembris |

*The Ancient Romans had a very different way of writing dates. Their system is explained on page 48.

# Colours and numbers

Colours are adjectives (describing words). They have endings like **-us**, **-a**, **-um** and **-er**, **-a**, **-um**, which change according to the noun they are describing.

## The colours

| ruber -bra, -brum | caeruleus, -a, -um | flavus, -a, -um | viridis, -is, -e | luteus, -a, -um | roseus, -a, -um | niger, -gra, -grum | albus, -a, -um | canus, -a, -um | fuscus, -a, -um |

## What colour is it?

Cover up the picture above and see if can you say what colour everything is in the painting. (You can check the answers on page 45.)

## Numbers

| 1 | unus | 11 | úndecim | 21 | vigínti unus | 31 | trigínta unus* |
|---|------|----|---------|----|--------------|----|----------------|
| 2 | duo | 12 | duódecim | 22 | vigínti duo | 40 | quádraginta |
| 3 | tres | 13 | trédecim | 23 | vigínti tres | 50 | quínquaginta |
| 4 | quáttuor | 14 | quattuórdecim | 24 | vigínti quattuor | 60 | séxaginta |
| 5 | quinque | 15 | quíndecim | 25 | vigínti quinque | 70 | séptuaginta |
| 6 | sex | 16 | sédecim | 26 | vigínti sex | 80 | óctoginta |
| 7 | septem | 17 | septéndecim | 27 | vigínti septem | 90 | nónaginta |
| 8 | octo | 18 | duodevigínti | 28 | duodetrigínta | 100 | centum |
| 9 | novem | 19 | undevigínti | 29 | undetrigínta | 200 | ducénti, -ae, -a |
| 10 | decem | 20 | vigínti | 30 | trigínta | 1000 | mille |

*The rest of the numbers from 32 to 99 are formed in the same way, so you can work them out for yourself. **duo-de**... means "two from..." and **un-de**... means "one from...".

# Pronunciation and grammar

Nobody knows exactly what Latin sounded like when the Ancient Romans spoke it. Today Latin is pronounced slightly differently in different parts of the world. In English-speaking countries, the letters are usually pronounced as they are written. There are a few exceptions: **"c"** is always pronounced "k", **"v"** is pronounced "w", and **"i"** before a vowel at the beginning of a word is pronounced "y". For example, **iam** is pronounced "yam". In some books, this **"i"** is printed "j", so it would be written **jam**, but is still pronounced "y".

## Accentuation

In words of two syllables, such as **mensa**, the stress is put on the first syllable. In this book, words with more than two syllables have an accent mark over the syllable that needs to be stressed, like this: **música**. The stress is never on the last syllable. You should not write this accent, though. It is just there to help you pronounce the word.

## Conjugation of verbs

The endings of Latin verbs change according to time (whether it is in the past, present or future) and person (I, you, we etc.). This is called conjugation. The unchanging part of the verb is called the stem.

There are four regular types of verbs: those with an **"a"** stem (such as **ama-re**), those with an **"e"** stem (such as **habe-re**), those with a hard letter (or consonant) stem (such as (**leg-ere**), and those with an **"i"** stem (such as **audi-re**).

Personal pronouns (I, you, we etc) are not usual in Latin. You can tell which person it is by the verb ending. The endings are:

| | | | |
|---|---|---|---|
| **-o/m** | I | **-mus** | we |
| **-s** | you | **-tis** | you (pl) |
| **-t** | he/she/it | **-nt** | they |

Here are the four main types of verbs in the present tense.

### 1. The "a" stem    2. The "e" stem

| **amare** | to love | **habere** | to have |
|---|---|---|---|
| **am-o** | I love | **habe-o** | I have |
| **ama-s** | you love | **habe-s** | you have |
| **ama-t** | he/she/it loves | **habe-t** | he/she/it has |
| **ama-mus** | we love | **habe-mus** | we have |
| **ama-tis** | you love | **habe-tis** | you have |
| **ama-nt** | they love | **habe-nt** | they have |

### 3. The consonant stem    4. The "i" stem

| **legere** | to read | **audire** | to hear |
|---|---|---|---|
| **leg-o** | I read | **audi-o** | I hear |
| **leg-i-s** | you read | **audi-s** | you hear |
| **leg-i-t** | he/she/it reads | **audi-t** | he/she/it hears |
| **leg-i-mus** | we read | **audi-mus** | we hear |
| **leg-i-tis** | you read | **audi-tis** | you hear |
| **leg-unt** | they read | **audi-u-nt** | they hear |

The verb "to be"

| **esse** | to be | | |
|---|---|---|---|
| **su-m** | I am | **su-mus** | we are |
| **e-s** | you are | **es-tis** | you are |
| **es-t** | he/she/it is | **su-nt** | they are |

## Imperative forms

| | 'a' conj. | 'e' conj. | 'cons.' conj. | 'i' conj. |
|---|---|---|---|---|
| Sing. | **ama** | **habe** | **lege** | **audi** |
| Plur. | **amáte** | **habéte** | **légite** | **audíte** |

# More grammar

## The future

The future tense of the 1st and 2nd conjugations is formed by adding **-bo**, **-bis**, **-bit** to the stem:

| | |
|---|---|
| **ama-b-o** | I shall love |
| **ama-b-is** | you will love |
| **ama-b-it** | he/she/it will love |
| **ama-bi-mus** | we shall love |
| **ama-bi-tis** | you will love |
| **ama-bu-nt** | they will love |
| | |
| **habe-b-o** | I shall have |
| **habe-bi-s** | you will have |
| **habe-bi-t** | he/she/it will have |
| **habe-bi-mus** | we shall have |
| **habe-bi-tis** | you will have |
| **habe-bu-nt** | they will have |

The future tense of 3rd and 4th conjugation verbs is formed by adding **-am**, **-es**, **-et** to the stem:

| | |
|---|---|
| **leg-a-m** | I shall read |
| **leg-e-s** | you will read |
| **leg-e-t** | he/she/it will read |
| **leg-e-mus** | we shall read |
| **leg-e-tis** | you will read |
| **leg-e-nt** | they will read |
| | |
| **audi-a-m** | I shall hear |
| **audi-e-s** | you will hear |
| **audi-e-t** | he/she/it will hear |
| **audi-e-mus** | we shall hear |
| **audi-e-tis** | you will hear |
| **audi-e-nt** | they will hear |

## Declension and cases

The change in the endings of nouns, pronouns and adjectives is called declension. The different endings are called cases. Here are the names of the cases and a rough guide to their uses.

| | |
|---|---|
| Nominative | For the subject of a sentence |
| Vocative | To speak to someone |
| Accusative | For the object of a sentence |
| Genitive | Used for "of" |
| Dative | Used for "to" or "for" |
| Ablative | Used for "by", "with", and "from". |

The vocative has the same ending as the nominative, except with 2nd declension singular nouns ending in **-us**. The vocative ending for those is **-e**, e.g. **serve**! (slave!)

## 1st declension nouns

Example: **mensa**  a table

| | Singular | Plural |
|---|---|---|
| Nom. | **mens-a** | **mens-ae** |
| Acc. | **mens-am** | **mens-as** |
| Gen. | **mens-ae** | **mens-arum** |
| Dat. | **mens-ae** | **mens-is** |
| Abl. | **mens-a** | **mens-is** |

## 2nd declension nouns

This declension includes nouns ending in **-us** and **-er** and neuter nouns ending in **-um**. Examples are **ann-us** (a year), **pu-er** (a boy) and **tect-um** (a roof).

| | Singular | Plural |
|---|---|---|
| Nom. | **ann-us** | **ann-i** |
| Voc. | **ann-e** | **ann-i** |
| Acc. | **ann-um** | **ann-os** |
| Gen. | **ann-i** | **ann-orum** |
| Dat. | **ann-o** | **ann-is** |
| Abl. | **ann-o** | **ann-is** |

Nouns ending in **-er** are different only in the nominative singular.

| | Singular | Plural |
|---|---|---|
| Nom. | **tect-um** | **tect-a** |
| Acc. | **tect-um** | **tect-a** |
| Gen. | **tect-i** | **tect-orum** |
| Dat. | **tect-o** | **tect-is** |
| Abl. | **tect-o** | **tect-is** |

In all neuter words, the ending of the accusative case (singular and plural) is the same as the ending of the nominative case.

# 3rd declension nouns

These nouns can be masculine, feminine or neuter. They have many different forms in the nominative singular.

Example: **canis**, **-is (m)** a dog

| | Singular | Plural |
|---|---|---|
| Nom. | **canis** | **can-es** |
| Acc. | **can-em** | **can-es** |
| Gen. | **can-is** | **can-um** |
| Dat. | **can-i** | **can-ibus** |
| Acc. | **can-e** | **can-ibus** |

Example: **aestas**, **-atis (f)** summer

| | Singular | Plural |
|---|---|---|
| Nom. | **aestas** | **aestat-es** |
| Acc. | **aestat-em** | **aestat-es** |
| Gen. | **aestat-is** | **aestat-um** |
| Dat. | **aestat-i** | **aestat-ibus** |
| Abl. | **aestat-e** | **aestat-ibus** |

# 1st and 2nd declension adjectives

These adjectives have the same feminine endings as nouns of the 1st declension. They have the same masculine and neuter endings as nouns of the 2nd declension.

Example: **bonus**, **-a**, **-um**, good

| | Singular Masculine | Feminine | Neuter |
|---|---|---|---|
| Nom. | **bon-us** | **bon-a** | **bon-um** |
| Voc. | **bon-e** | **bon-a** | **bon-um** |
| Acc. | **bon-um** | **bon-am** | **bon-um** |
| Gen. | **bon-i** | **bon-ae** | **bon-i** |
| Dat. | **bon-o** | **bon-ae** | **bon-o** |
| Abl. | **bon-o** | **bon-a** | **bon-o** |

| | Plural Masculine | Feminine | Neuter |
|---|---|---|---|
| Nom. | **bon-i** | **bon-ae** | **bon-a** |
| Acc. | **bon-os** | **bon-as** | **bon-a** |
| Gen. | **bon-orum** | **bon-arum** | **bon-orum** |
| Dat. | **bon-is** | **bon-is** | **bon-is** |
| Abl. | **bon-is** | **bon-is** | **bon-is** |

# 3rd declension adjectives

These adjectives all end in **-is** in the genitive singular. There are three groups. The plural is the same in all of them.

**Group 1** (3 endings in the nom. sing.)

Example: **acer**, **-is**   sharp, fierce

| | Singular Masculine | Feminine | Neuter |
|---|---|---|---|
| Nom. | **acer** | **acris** | **acre** |
| Acc. | **acrem** | **acrem** | **acre** |
| Gen. | **acris** | **acris** | **acris** |
| Dat. | **acri** | **acri** | **acri** |
| Abl. | **acri** | **acri** | **acri** |

| | Plural Masculine | Feminine | Neuter |
|---|---|---|---|
| Nom. | **acres** | **acres** | **acria** |
| Acc. | **acres** | **acres** | **acria** |
| Gen. | **acrium** | **acrium** | **acrium** |
| Dat. | **acribus** | **acribus** | **acribus** |
| Abl. | **acribus** | **acribus** | **acribus** |

**Group 2** (2 endings in nom. sing.)

Example: **fortis**, **-is**   brave, strong

| | Singular Masculine | Feminine | Neuter |
|---|---|---|---|
| Nom. | **fortis** | **fortis** | **forte** |
| Acc. | **fortem** | **fortem** | **forte** |
| Gen. | **fortis** | **fortis** | **fortis** |
| Dat. | **forti** | **forti** | **forti** |
| Abl. | **forti** | **forti** | **forti** |

**Group 3** (1 ending in nom. sing.)

Example: **felix**, **-icis**   happy, lucky

| | Singular Masculine | Feminine | Neuter |
|---|---|---|---|
| Nom. | **felix** | **felix** | **felix** |
| Acc. | **felicem** | **felicem** | **felix** |
| Gen. | **felicis** | **felicis** | **felicis** |
| Dat. | **felici** | **felici** | **felici** |
| Abl. | **felici** | **felici** | **felici** |

# Answers to puzzles

Page 7

## What are they called?

nomen eius Petrus est.
nomen eius Claudia est.
nomina eorum Paulus et Petrus sunt.
nomen meum est...

## Who is who?

Lucius is speaking to Quintus.
Cornelia is speaking to Beata.
Lucius is swimming, bottom right, with a
    green bathing-cap.
Quintus is talking to him.
Carolus is reading the paper.
The man saying "good-bye" to Carolus.

## Can you remember?

quod nomen tibi est?
nomen meum est ...
haec amica mea est. nomen eius Beata est.
hic amicus meus est. nomen eius Gaius est.

Page 9

## Can you remember?

hic flos est. haec feles est.
haec arbor est. hic nidus est.
haec avis est. haec domus est.
hic sol est. haec fenestra est.
hoc autocineticum est. hic canis est.

Page 11

## Who comes from where?

Franciscus comes from Austria.
Arius and Indira.
Lolita is Spanish.
Janus lives in Hungary.
Yes, Angus comes from Scotland.
Marie and Pierre come from France.
Budapest is in Hungary.

## Can you remember?

unde venis.                venio e/ex...
scio loqui Latine.         scisne loqui Latine?

Page 13

## How old are they?

Afer is 13.                Livia is 11.
Diana and Sylvia are 15.   Lucius is 9.
Titus is 12.               Aemilia is 5.

## Brothers and sisters

A = Diana et Sylvia  B = Lucius  C = Afer
D = Titus  E = Livia

Page 17

## Where is everyone?

avus in cenaculo est.
Quintus in coquina est.
Petrus in balneo est.
mater in cubiculo est.

avia in mediano est.
larva in cubiculo Isabellae est.
Isabella in summo tabulato est.
Petrus in balneo est.

## Can you remember?

ego in urbe habito, tu ruri. cubiculum in
summo tabulato est. avia in insula habitat.
Quintus est in balneo. habitamus in domo.

Page 19

## Where are the animals hiding?

cricetus in vasculo est.
feles parva post televisorium est.
canicula in armario est.
psittacus in librario est.
serpens sub sponda est.
testudo prope telephonum est.

Page 21

## Who likes what

Henricus caseum amat.
Marcus pernam non amat.
avus uvas praefert.
amo/non amo...

44

## Who is saying what?

"esurio!"
"bene tibi sapiat."
"sume aliquid, quaeso!"
"potesne mihi dare hyalum?"
"visne etiam poma terrestria assa?"
"volo."
"nolo. satis est."
"optime sapit."

## What are they doing?

A coquit B natat C saltant D violina canit
E pingit

## Questions and answers

| quid facis? | coquo. |
| quid facis? | nato. |
| quid facitis? | saltamus. |
| quid facis? | violina cano. |
| quid facis? | pingo. |

## Marcus's day

1B, 2E, 3F, 4A, 5H, 6G, 7D, 8C.

## What is the time?

A   quinque minutis post tertiam horam.
B   quinque minutis post undecimam horam.
C   octo minutis ante nonam horam.
D   quadrante ante quartam horam.
E   viginti quinque minutis post tertiam horam.
F   septima hora et dimidia.
G   tertia hora.
H   quarta hora.
I   nona hora.
J   prima hora et dimidia.
K   quinque minutis post septimam horam.
L   decima hora et dimidia.
M   sexta hora.
N   viginti quinque minutis ante quartam horam.
O   septem minutis ante secundam horam.

## Your diary for the week

vesperi saltabo cum Tito.
die Lunae, Mercurii, Solis teniludio ludo.
die Martis secunda hora clavario cano.

## In Messina

qua via ad forum venio/adibo? da mihi veniam, estne cafea in propinquo? cape tertiam viam a dextra, deinde vehere semper in directum. cape tertiam viam a sinistra, deinde vehere semper in directum.

To the school.

## Buying fruit

requiro quattuor citrea, unam libram bananarum et unam ananasam. quattuor citrea constant sexaginta sestertiis, una libra bananarum constat quinquaginta octo sestertiis, et una ananasa constat centum decem sestertiis. omnia constant ducentis quinquaginta sestertiis. una ananasa una libra persicarum. tria arancia constant sexaginta sex sestertiis. una libra malorum constat quinquaginta quinque sestertiis.

## When is your birthday?

natalis Roberti est die vicesmo primo m.Iunii.
natalis Helenae est die duodevicesmo m. Octobris.
natalis Clarae est die tricesimo primo m. Augusti.
natalis Claudii est die tertio m. Martii.
natalis Leonis est die septimo m. Septembris.

## What colour is it?

via cana est. sol flavus est. tectum luteum est. caelum caeruleum est. flores rosei sunt. canis fuscus est. avis nigra est. autocineticum rubrum est. arbores virides sunt. domus alba est.

# Vocabulary

The nouns are shown with both their nominative and genitive endings. For example: **mensa, -ae** (f) table. **mensa** is nominative, **mensae** is genitive and (f) means the noun is feminine.

The other abbreviations are adv. (adverb), pl. (plural), pr. (present tense), irr. (irregular), acc. (accusative), and abl. (ablative).

Adjectives are shown in the nominative singular, with the masculine ending followed by the feminine and neuter ones. For example: **fuscus, -a, -um** brown.

Verbs are shown in the first person singular (I...), followed by the infinitive (to...). The declension number is also shown. For example: **amo/amare** 1 to love.

| | | | |
|---|---|---|---|
| **a sinistra parte** | on the left side | **citreum, -i** (n) | lemon |
| **ad + acc.** | at, to | **clavarium, -i** (n) | piano |
| **adeo/adire** (irr.) | to go to | **cola, -ae** (f) | cola |
| **aestas, -atis** (f) | summer | **contra** + acc. | opposite, against |
| **aliquid** | something | | |
| **amo/amare** 1 | to love | **coquo/coquere** 3 | to cook |
| **amica, -ae** (f) | friend | **crassus, -a, -um** | thick, fat |
| **amicus, -i** (m) | friend | **cricetus, -i** (m) | hamster |
| **amita, -ae** (f) | aunt (father's sister) | **cubiculum, -i** (n) | bedroom |
| | | **cum** + abl. | with |
| **ananasa, -ae** (f) | pineapple | **curia, -ae** (f) | town hall |
| **Anglice** | in English | | |
| **annus, -i** (m) | year | **do/dare** 1 | to give |
| **ante** + acc. | in front of, before | **decem** | ten |
| | | **December, -bris** (m) | December |
| **Aprilis, -ilis** (m) | April | **decimus, -a, -um** | tenth |
| **aqua, -ae** (f) | water | **deinde** | then |
| **aranciata, -ae** (f) | orangeade | **desidero/desiderare** 1 | to desire |
| **arancium, -i** (n) | an orange | **deversorium, -i** (n) | hotel |
| **arbor, -oris** (f) | tree | **deverticulum juvenum** (n) | youth hostel |
| **argentaria, -ae** (f) | bank | **dexter, -tra, -trum** | right (-hand) |
| **armarium, -i** (n) | cupboard | **dextrorsum** | to the right |
| **athletica, -ae** (f) | sport | **dic mihi** | tell me |
| **audio/audire** 4 | to hear | **dies, diei** (m) | day |
| **Augustus, -i** (m) | August | **dies Iovis** (m) | Thursday |
| **Austria, -ae** (f) | Austria | **dies Lunae** (m) | Monday |
| **aut** | or | **dies Martis** (m) | Tuesday |
| **autocineticum, i** (n) | motor car | **dies Mercurii** (m) | Wednesday |
| **autoraeda, -ae** (f) | motor car | **dies Solis** (m) | Sunday |
| **autumnus, -i** (m) | autumn | **dies Veneris** (m) | Friday |
| **avia, -ae** (f) | grandmother | **dimidius -a, -um** | half |
| **avis, is** (f) | bird | **discotheca** (f) | disco |
| **avunculus, -i** (m) | uncle (mother's brother) | **displicet mihi ...** | I don't like ... |
| | | **doleo/dolere** 2 quod.. | I am sorry that ... |
| **avus, -i** (m) | grandfather | | |
| | | **domus, -us** (f) | house |
| **balneum. -i** (n) | bath | **dormitum ire** | to go to bed |
| **banana, -ae** (f) | banana | **duo, duae, duo** | two |
| **bene** | well, good! | | |
| **bene tibi sapiat!** | bon appetit! | **e, ex** + abl. | from, out of |
| **bene valeo/valere** 2 | to be well | **ecce!** | here is, look! |
| **bonus, -a, -um** | good | **ecclesia, -ae** (f) | church |
| **botulus, -i** (m) | sausage | **edo/edere** 3 | to eat |
| **Britannia, -ae** (f) | Britain | **ego** | I |
| **bubula assa, -ae,** (f) | steak | **eius** | his, her, of him |
| **butyrum, -i** (n) | butter | **emo/emere** 3 | to buy |
| | | **eo/ire** (irr.) | to go |
| **cafea, -ae** (f) | café, coffee | **eorum** | their, of them |
| **caminus, -i** (m) | chimney | **ergo** | then, therefore |
| **canicula, -ae** (f) | puppy | **esurio/esurire** 4 | to be hungry |
| **canis, -is** (m) | dog | **etiam** | also, even |
| **cano, canere** 3 | to play | | |
| **caseus, -i** (m) | cheese | **facio/facere** 3 | to do, to make |
| **cena, -ae** (f) | dinner | **familia, -ae** (f) | family, household |
| **cenaculum** (n) | dining room | | |
| **chartula, -ae** (f) | postcard | **Februarius, -i** (m) | February |
| **chiliogrammum, -i** (n) | kilogram | **feles, is** (f) | cat |
| **cibaria,-orum** (n.pl.) | food | **fenestra, -ae** (f) . | window |
| **cinema, -ae** (f) | cinema | **fere** | almost, about |

| | | | |
|---|---|---|---|
| **flavus, -a, -um** | blond, yellow | | |
| **flecte te** | turn! | | |
| **flos, floris** (m) | flower | | |
| **frater, -tris** (m) | brother | | |
| **fuscus, -a, -um** | dark, brown | | |
| **Germania, -ae** (f) | Germany | | |
| **Germanice** | (in) German | | |
| **glacies, -iei** (f) | ice, an ice | | |
| **gratias ago/agere** 3 | to thank | | |
| **gracilis, -is, -e** | thin | | |
| **habeo/habere** 2 | to have | | |
| **habito/habitare** 1 | to live in | | |
| **Hammaburgensis, -is** (m) | hamburger | | |
| **Helvetia, -ae** (f) | Switzerland | | |
| **hic, haec, hoc** | this | | |
| **hiems, hiemis** (f) | winter | | |
| **Hispania, -ae** (f) | Spain | | |
| **hodie** | today | | |
| **holus, -eris** (n) | vegetable | | |
| **hora, -ae** (f) | hour | | |
| **Hungaria, -ae** (f) | Hungary | | |
| **hyalus, -i** (m) | a glass | | |
| **Ianuarius, -i** (m) | January | | |
| **ibi** | there | | |
| **ientaculum, -i** (n) | breakfast | | |
| **illic** | there | | |
| **in** + acc. | into, onto | | |
| **in** + abl. | in, on | | |
| **in directum** | straight ahead | | |
| **in propinquo** | nearby | | |
| **India, -ae** (f) | India | | |
| **instrumentum musicum, -i,** (n) | musical instrument | | |
| **inter** + acc. | among, between | | |
| **ire** (pr. tense eo) | to go | | |
| **is, ea, id** | that | | |
| **ita** | so, thus | | |
| **ita est** | yes | | |
| **Iulius, -i** (m) | July | | |
| **Iunius, -i** (m) | June | | |
| **lac, lactis** (n) | milk | | |
| **lactuca, -ae** (f) | lettuce, salad | | |
| **laniena, -ae** (f) | butcher's (shop) | | |
| **larva, -ae** (f) | ghost | | |
| **Latine** | (in) Latin | | |
| **lego/legere** 3 | to read | | |
| **libra, -ae** (f) | a pound (weight) | | |
| **librarium, -i** (n) | bookcase | | |
| **limonata, -ae** (f) | lemonade | | |
| **Londini** | in London | | |
| **longinquus, -a, -um** | distant, far away | | |
| **loquor/loqui** 3 dep. | to talk | | |

46

|  |  |
|---|---|
| ludo/ludere 3 | to play (a game) |
| Lutetiae | in Paris |
| magnus, -a, um | large, big |
| Maius, -i (m) | May |
| malum, -i (n) | apple |
| mane (adv. & noun) | (in the) morning |
| mare, maris (n) | sea |
| Martius, -i (m) | March |
| mater, -tris (f) | mother |
| matertera, -ae (f) | aunt (mother's sister) |
| maxime | very much, most |
| media nox, mediae noctis (f) | midnight |
| medianum, -i (n) | living-room |
| mensa, -ae (f) | table |
| mensis, -is (m) | month |
| meridies, -iei (m) | midday |
| meus, -a, -um | my |
| mihi (dat. of ego) | to me, for me |
| mihi est/sunt... | I have ... |
| mihi placet... | I like ... |
| minime | not at all, least |
| minuta, -ae (f) | minute |
| musica, -orum (n.pl) | music |
| nam | for |
| natalis, -is (m) | birthday |
| nato/natare 1 | to swim |
| natus, -a, -um | born (old) |
| -ne | (asks a question) |
| neque ... neque | neither ... nor |
| nidus, -i (m) | nest |
| nihil laboris est | it's no trouble |
| nolo/nolle (irr.) | I do not want |
| nomen, -inis (n) | name |
| non | not |
| nonus, -a, -um | ninth |
| novem | nine |
| November, -bris (m) | November |
| octavus, -a, -um | eighth |
| officium postale (n) | Post Office |
| omnia, -ium (n. pl) | everything |
| optime | very good, excellent |
| oryza, -ae (f) | rice |
| ovum, -i (n) | egg |
| paene | almost, nearly |
| palatium, -i (n) | palace |
| panicellus, -i (m) | roll, bun |
| panis, -is (m) | bread |
| parentes, -ium (m) | parents |
| pars, partis (f) | part |
| parvus, -a, -um | small, little |
| pasta vermiculata -ae, -ae (f) | spaghetti |
| pater, -tris (m) | father |
| patruus, -i (m) | uncle (father's brother) |
| paulum (adv.) | a little |
| pedibus | on foot, walking |
| pedifollis, -is (m) | football |
| pediludium -i (n) | football |
| perna, -ae (f) | ham |
| persicum, -i (n) | peach |
| pessime (adv.) | very bad, terrible |
| phamacopola, -ae (f) | chemist's (shop) |
| pingo/pingere 3 | to paint |
| piscina, -ae (f) | swimming pool |
| pitta, -ae (f) | pizza |
| placenta, -ae (f) | cake |
| planta, -ae (f) | plant |
| plasso/plassare 1 | to make models |
| poma terrestria assa (n.pl) | chips |
| pomum, -i (n) | fruit |
| porta, -ae (f) | door, gate |
| possum/posse (irr.) | to be able |
| post + acc. | behind, after |
| potus socolatae (m) | chocolate drink |
| praefectura (-ae) commeatus (f) | travel information bureau |
| praefero/-ferre (irr.) | to prefer |
| prandium, -i (n) | lunch |
| primus, -a, -um | first |
| pistrina, -ae (f) | bakery |
| prope + acc. | near |
| proximus, -a, -um | next, nearest |
| puella, -ae (f) | girl |
| puer, -i (m) | boy |
| qua via? | by what road? how? |
| quadrans, -ntis (m) | a quarter |
| quaero/quaerere 3 | to look for, ask |
| quaeso | please |
| quando? | when? |
| quanti constat/ constant ...? | how much does...cost? |
| quartus, -a, -um | fourth |
| quattuor | four |
| que | and |
| qui dies hodie est? | what day is it today? |
| quid? | what? |
| quid aliud? | what else? |
| quinque | five |
| quintus, -a, -um | fifth |
| quis? | who? |
| quod nomen? | what name? |
| quoque | also |
| quot? | how many? |
| quota hora est? | what time is it? |
| ratio, -ionis (f) | bill |
| reperio/reperire 4 | to find |
| requiro/requirere 3 | to want |
| Romae | in Rome |
| rosa, -ae (f) | rose |
| ruri | in the country |
| saeptum, -i (n) | fence |
| salto/saltare 1 | to dance |
| salve! | hello! |
| sapio/sapere 3 | to taste |
| sapitne bene? | does it taste good? |
| satis (adv.) | enough |
| schola, -ae (f) | school |
| scio/scire 4 | to know (how to...) |
| scriblita, -ae (f) | a tart |
| secundus, -a, -um | second |
| sed | but |
| sella, -ae (f) | armchair |
| septem | seven |
| September, -bris (m) | September |
| septimus, -a, -um | seventh |
| sex | six |
| sextus, -a, -um | sixth |
| sinister, -tra, -trum | left |
| sol, -is (m) | sun |
| soror, -oris (f) | sister |
| specto/spectare 1 | to look at, gaze at |
| sponda, -ae (f) | sofa |
| stabulum autocinetum (n) | garage |
| statio ferriviaria (f) | railway station |
| sub + abl. | under |
| sum/esse (irr.) | to be |
| supermercatus, -us (m) | supermarket |
| surgo/surgere 3 | to rise |
| taberna, -ae (f) | shop, tavern |
| taberna alimentaria (f) | grocer's (shop) |
| tabulatum, -i (n) | storey |
| tapete, -is (n) | carpet |
| tectum, -i (n) | roof |
| telephonum, -i (n) | telephone |
| televisorium, -i (n) | television |
| tener, -era, -erum | gentle |
| teniludium, -i (n) | tennis |
| tertius, -a, -um | third |
| texo/texere 3 | to weave, knit |
| thea, -ae (f) | tea |
| tibi (dat. of tu) | to you, for you |
| tibi est/sunt... | you have ... |
| tomata, -ae (f) | tomato |
| tres, tres, tria | three |
| tu (acc. = te) | you (singular) |
| tum | then |
| tuus, -a, -um | your |
| ubi? | where? |
| unde? | where from? |
| unus, -a, -um | one |
| urbis, urbis (f) | city |
| usque ad diem crastinum | until tomorrow |
| ut | how |
| uva, -ae (f) | grape |
| valde | very much |
| vale! | goodbye! |
| valeo/valere 3 | to be well |
| vasculum, -i (n) | vase |
| vehere! | drive! |
| velim | I would like |
| velum, -i (n) | curtain, sail |
| venio/venire 4 | to come |
| ver, -is (n) | spring |
| vesperi | in the evening |
| vestibulum, -i (n) | entrance hall |
| veterrimus, -a, -um | very old, oldest |
| via, -ae (f) | road, street |
| vicesmus, -a, -um | twentieth |
| viginti | twenty |
| violina, -ae (f) | violin |
| volo/velle (irr.) | to want |
| visne? | do you want? |

# Numbers, dates and time

## How the Romans told the time

The Romans divided the daylight, from sunrise to sunset, into twelve equal hours. These hours varied in length as the days became longer or shorter, depending on the time of year. **hora prima** always started at sunrise, and **hora septima** always started at midday. The night was divided into four equal **vigiliae** (meaning "watches"). **vigilia prima** was from sunset to approximately 9 p.m. **vigilia tertia** always started at midnight. The Romans only had water clocks and sun dials to help them tell the time, and these were not very convenient.

## Roman Numbers

The signs the Romans used for numbers were **I** (one), **V** (five), **X** (ten), **L** (50), **C** (100), **D** (500), **M** (1000).

In most cases, you can identify the other numbers by adding the signs together. This works for signs of equal value next to each other. For example, **III** = 3 and **CCC** = 300. It also works if the sign of a larger value is followed by a smaller one. For example, **VIII** = 8, **XXVII** = 27, **LXI** = 61, and **CCLVII** = 257.

But if a sign is followed by one of a larger value, the first sign is subtracted from the second, larger one. For example, **IV**= 4, (**I** is subtracted from **V**), **IX** = 9, **XLIV** = 44, **XC** = 90, **CM** = 900, **MCM** = 1900, **MCMXCIII** = 1993.

Can you work out what these numbers are: **XXXIX**, **CCXLVII**, **MLXVI**, **MDCCXXIV**, **MMMDCCLXXIX**?

How would you write these numbers in Roman numerals: 17, 59, 385, 1,234, 4,321?

## Roman dates

The names of the different months of the year come from the names the Romans used. After the time of Julius Caesar, the Roman months were the same as ours, except that they had no leap year, and no names for days and weeks. There were three fixed times in each month. The first day of the month was always called the **Kalends**. For most months of the year, the fifth day was called the **Nones** and the thirteenth day was called the **Ides**. But in March, May, July and October, the **Nones** and **Ides** were the seventh and fifteenth days.

The Romans described the date in relation to the next fixed point. So, for example, January 31st was "the day before the Kalends of February". They wrote this as **pridie KAL. FEB.**
The Romans included the days on which they started and finished counting. So January 30th was "three days before the Kalends of February", or "the third day-before the Kalends of February" : **antediem tertium KAL. FEB.** This was usually abbreviated to **a.d.III KAL. FEB.**

Here are a few more examples:

February 1st was **KAL. FEB.** February 2nd was **a.d.IV NON. FEB** (four days before the Nones). February 4th was **pridie NON. FEB.** February 5th was **NON. FEB.** February 6th was **a.d.VIII ID. FEB.**

See if you can translate these modern dates into Roman ones: March 15, April 3, June 10, July 24, October 6, November 1. The answers are at the bottom of the page. (Note: **Ides** were abbreviated to **ID.**)

## Answers:

Roman numbers: 39, 247, 1066, 1724, 3779: **XVII, LIX, CCCLXXXV, MCCXXXIV, MMMMCCCXXI.**

Roman dates: **ID. MAR.; a.d.III NON. APR.; a.d.IV ID JUN.; a.d.IX KAL. AUG.; pridie NON. OCT.; KAL. NOV.**

First published in 1993 by Usborne Publishing Ltd, 83-85 Saffron Hill, London EC1N 8RT, England. www.usborne.com